IN THEIR OWN WORDS

WORLD WAR II

A Primary Source History

Colin Hynson

GARETH**STEVENS**
PUBLISHING
A Member of the WRC Media Family of Companies

Cover photos:
Top: *During World War II, U.S. General Dwight D. Eisenhower was the head of U.S. forces in Europe. In 1942, he was made commander of Allied forces in North Africa and Supreme Allied commander in Europe. In 1952, he was elected to the office of president of the United States.*
Bottom: *U.S. warplanes on a bombing run over Europe.*

CONTENTS

World War II, the largest and most destructive war in human history, gripped the world between 1939 and 1945. Never before had so many people—military and civilian—been caught up in the horrors of warfare. People in nearly every country suffered from the war. This six-year conflict ended with the complete destruction of two cities by a new type of weapon that remains controversial to this day. The end of World War II also saw the rise of the Soviet Union and the United States of America as the two world superpowers.

The main reason for World War II (WWII) goes back to the way World War I (WWI) ended in 1918. Germany, Italy, and Japan came out of WWI resentful about the way that the Allied Forces of France, Britain, and the United States had treated them. This resentment eventually led to the rise of governments determined to make up for what they believed they had lost in 1918. In the following two decades, dictators rose to power in Germany and Italy. In Japan, the military kept a firm grip on the civilian government. World War II began on September 1, 1939, when the German army invaded Poland. Two days later, Britain and France declared war on Germany.

Below: *During World War II, men from the Home Guard, like these from Treeton, England, supplemented the British army.*

By the summer of 1940, the Germans and their Italian allies controlled much of Europe. On June 22, 1941, the war spread even further when Germany invaded the Soviet Union.

At that point, the war was confined to Europe and to some limited battles in North Africa. That changed on December 7, 1941, when the Japanese attacked the American Pacific Fleet stationed at Pearl Harbor in Hawaii. The United States declared war on Japan the next day.

Left: *Although aircraft were used in World War I, air power was used to an unprecedented extent during World War II.*

Above: *Airborne Allied soldiers get ready for action during 1943.*

Below: *Women assumed traditional mens' duties as the men left to fight the war. The distinctive uniform of the "Land Girls" became a familiar sight on Britain's farms.*

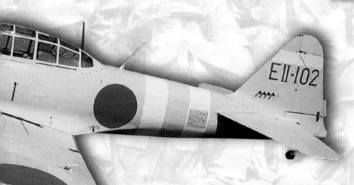

When Germany and Italy declared war on the United States on December 11, 1941, the conflict stretched across the world. At first, the Germans, Italians, and Japanese (the "Axis" powers), did well. France had fallen and Britain faced Germany alone. The attack on the Soviet Union was swift, and by the end of December 1941, the German army was approaching Moscow. In Asia and the Pacific, the Japanese conquered Burma (now Myanmar), Hong Kong, the Philippines, and Singapore, and threatened both India and Australia.

At the start of 1942, battle outcomes began to change. The cold Russian winter helped the Soviet Army push the Germans out of the Soviet Union. In June 1942, the Battle of Midway halted the Japanese advance in the Pacific. By the end of 1942, the Axis

Above: *Everyday provisions, such as tea and coffee, were limited and subject to rationing during WWII.*

Below: *Field Marshal Erwin Rommel fought for Germany in World War I. In WWII, he led a German Panzer Division during the 1940 invasion of France.*

powers were rapidly losing territories they had gained. The Axis simply could not match the combined military and industrial strength of the Soviet Union and the United States. On June 6, 1944, Allied troops landed on the beaches of Normandy on the north coast of France. The invasion marked the beginning of the end, for the Germans were now fighting on two fronts. Germany surrendered on May 8, 1945. France, Britain, the United States, and the Soviet Union divided up control over the former German territories. In Asia and the Pacific, American forces slowly pushed back the Japanese. U.S. forces began "island-hopping"— taking back selected islands in the Pacific with the goal of establishing a West Pacific air base from which U.S. bombers could attack the Japanese mainland. In November 1944, heavy air attacks on Japanese cities began. This culminated in the dropping of atomic bombs on Hiroshima and Nagasaki on August 6 and 9, 1945, respectively. The Japanese surrendered informally on August 14, 1945, and signed the formal, unconditional surrender on September 2, 1945. World War II was over.

Above: *A scene from the movie Saving Private Ryan, set in World War II. The beginning of the movie, which shows U.S. forces landing on Omaha Beach on D-Day, is a brutally realistic portrayal of the violence of war.*

The world in 1945 was very different from the one that had existed in 1939. The British and the French lost much of their power and influence, and the empires that they each held began falling apart. Countries in Eastern Europe fell under the control of the Soviet Union. China collapsed into a civil war that resulted in victory for the communists. The United States emerged from the war with its territories intact and grew into a global power. This led to the start of the Cold War between the United States and the Soviet Union. The Cold War lasted until the late 1980s. Relationships between East and West have improved since then.

Above: *A plaque on France's Normandy Coast commemorates Colonel Rudder's Rangers, an elite fighting unit that scaled the cliffs of Pointe du Hoc on D-Day to capture a German gun fortification. The Rangers sustained heavy casualties that day.*

Other factors, such as the fear of international terrorism in the wake of the terrorist attacks of September 11, 2001, now take center stage.

Right: *The devastation left by the dropping of an atomic bomb on the Japanese city of Hiroshima on August 6, 1945. The bombing of Nagasaki three days later effectively ended WWII.*

The origins of World War II can be traced back to mistakes made at the end of World War I. That earlier conflict pitted Britain, France, Russia, Italy, and the United States against Germany, Austria-Hungary, Turkey, and Bulgaria. The war started in July 1914 and ended in November 1918 with the defeat of Germany and its allies. As the years passed, the grievances of entire nations—combined with the hardships of economic depression—created aggressive governments determined to win back what they felt was rightfully theirs.

Above: The bronze World War I Victory medal awarded by the United States. All fourteen allied nations used the same double-rainbow ribbon, but the pendant design differed by nation.

"In spite of such monstrous demands, the rebuilding of our economic system is at the same time made impossible. We are to surrender our merchant fleet. We are to give up all foreign interests. We are to transfer to our opponents the property of all German undertakings abroad. ... Even after the conclusion of peace, the enemy states are to be empowered to confiscate all German property."

German foreign minister who signed the Treaty of Versailles.

THE END OF WORLD WAR I

Representatives from the victorious countries met at the Palace of Versailles near Paris, France, in January 1919 to discuss the peace treaty with Germany.

The Germans were not invited to participate in these discussions, but they were forced to sign the final treaty in June 1919. The Treaty of Versailles demanded that Germany drastically reduce the size of its armed forces. The army was cut to one hundred thousand men confined to German land east of the Rhine River. The German Navy was reduced to just twenty-four ships, and Germany was forbidden to have an air force. On top of that, the Germans lost land to bordering countries and had to forfeit their African and Asian colonies. The Germans also had to pay for the damage caused by the war in Europe. This amounted to the equivalent of about $1.5 billion. The Treaty of Versailles was designed to ensure that Germany would never again pose a military threat in Europe. The Treaty humiliated and angered the German people. They considered it unfair and felt that the victorious countries were interested only in revenge.

Left: A sharecropper from Virginia. The Great Depression hit every part of the economy hard, from big business to farming.

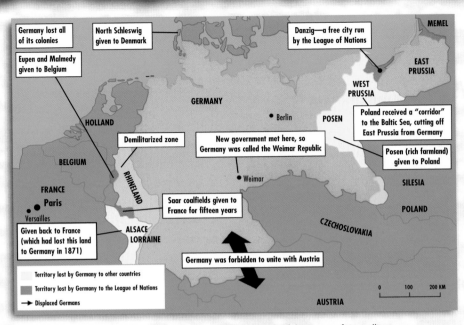

- Germany lost all of its colonies
- North Schleswig given to Denmark
- Eupen and Malmedy given to Belgium
- Danzig—a free city run by the League of Nations
- MEMEL
- EAST PRUSSIA
- WEST PRUSSIA
- GERMANY
- HOLLAND
- Berlin
- POSEN
- Poland received a "corridor" to the Baltic Sea, cutting off East Prussia from Germany
- Demilitarized zone
- New government met here, so Germany was called the Weimar Republic
- Posen (rich farmland) given to Poland
- BELGIUM
- RHINELAND
- Weimar
- SILESIA
- FRANCE
- Paris
- POLAND
- Versailles
- Saar coalfields given to France for fifteen years
- CZECHOSLOVAKIA
- Given back to France (which had lost this land to Germany in 1871)
- ALSACE LORRAINE
- Germany was forbidden to unite with Austria
- Territory lost by Germany to other countries
- Territory lost by Germany to the League of Nations
- Displaced Germans
- 0   100   200 KM
- AUSTRIA

Above: A map shows the territory lost by Germany as a result of the Treaty of Versailles.

TIME LINE 1918–1929

November 11, 1918
WWI Armistice signed at Compiègne, France.

June 28, 1919
Treaty of Versailles signed.

January 3, 1925
Mussolini dismisses Italian parliament and becomes dictator.

October 29, 1929
Wall Street Stock Market crashes.

Below: *The Treaty of Versailles was signed in the famous Hall of Mirrors in the Palace of Versailles.*

THE GREAT DEPRESSION

In October 1929, the world began sliding into a time of poor economic outlook known as the Great Depression. From 1929 to the middle of the 1930s, a worldwide lowering of economic options occurred. Trade between nations collapsed. Thousands of companies went out of business. Unemployment and poverty grew. Fourteen million people in the United States lost their jobs, and three million people in Britain were unemployed. More than six million people in Germany lost their jobs. Half the factories in Japan closed. People in many of the countries hit hard by the Depression began looking toward political leaders who promised jobs and stability. In Germany, Italy, and Japan, the new governments that came to power

"Sometimes during the winter . . . when the snow fell in Detroit, [Michigan], they called for people they wanted to shovel the snow, and of course everybody didn't get hired—you just had to go out there and the foreman would be throwing the shovel and if you happened to catch it you're hired. And so my father would go out there and on occasion he would be hired and earn a couple of dollars for the day's work. . . . Shoes, of course, were a problem and many times I remember I wore out the soles down to the pavement, so to speak, and you had to put cardboard in there."

Richard Waskin, who was four when the Great Depression hit the U.S. in 1929.

Above: *The Germany army marches in Poland during 1939.*

governments could solve the crisis of the Great Depression. They saw democratic governments as weak and unable to handle tough decisions. Between 1919 and 1922, Italy had five different governments. Street fights erupted between the Communists and a new political force called the Fascists. In October 1922, Fascist leader Benito Mussolini demanded that the Fascists should become the new Italian government. Faced with the possibility of civil war, people accepted his idea. Between 1924 and 1926, Mussolini made himself the dictator of Italy.

Mussolini adopted an aggressive foreign policy for Italy. He invaded Ethiopia in Africa in 1935 as the start of a new "Roman Empire."

not only promised to work for the people, but also pledged to make their countries strong again.

THE FAILURE OF DEMOCRACY

Many people felt that their democratic governments had failed them. The Treaty of Versailles humiliated the Germans. Although Italy and Japan had fought on the victorious side in WWI, the Treaty gave them very little. Some believed that only firm, strong

Right: *Adolf Hitler, pictured with the Italian fascist dictator Mussolini (on left).*

"When we got in, Hitler's speech was in progress on the radio and the Cowells were listening in. By missing some supper, I managed to hear most of it, although I only understood a word of it here and there.

"The Führer was arresting and theatrical, making the most of an emotional delivery. From what I could gather in fragments from the Cowells, he means no surrender. Sooner or later he will have Czechoslovakia; his armament and defenses will be ready before the autumn is out. In each pause, a crowd of thousands cheered and roared and howled. Hearing Hitler's very words and those frenzied howls brought home without doubt the terrible significance of it. Hitler means war."

The diary of Moyra Charlton from September 12, 1938. She later served with the British army as an ambulance driver.

Above: *A row of wrecked buildings in Boundary Road, Shanghai, China, during the Sino-Japanese War.*

TIME LINE
1931–1933

November 8, 1931
Franklin Delano Roosevelt elected president of the United States.

January 30, 1933
Hitler appointed chancellor of Germany.

July 14, 1933
Nazi party declared the official party of Germany.

EXPANSION IN JAPAN AND GERMANY

At the end of World War I, the Japanese received some land formerly controlled by the Germans. The Japanese felt that they should have been given more. The Depression also caused a lot of suffering in Japan. People in the armed forces blamed the "weakness" of their democratic government and believed the solution was to conquer foreign lands. That way, the Japanese factories would have

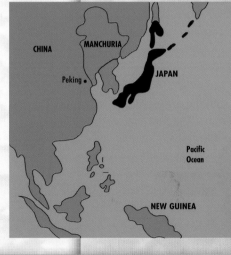

"For three months I had managed to avoid saluting the swastika flag. . . . I tried it once too often, however. . . . I caught sight of an approaching procession of Nazi nurses carrying banners. Without stopping to think, I turned my back on it and walked in the opposite direction, only to face four Brownshirts crossing towards me from the other side of the street.

'Trying to get out of it?' said one. 'Arm up!' And now? 'Heil Hitler,' I said.

I could have spat at myself as I strode past the procession with arm uplifted."

From All Quiet in Germany by Karl Billinger, published in 1935.

"During numerous raids today, the German airman have dropped thousands of articles of various kinds, including packets of food and sweets. The population have been warned not to touch any of these things. During one of the afternoon raids, the German bombers scattered Polish banknotes in large quantities; these were discovered to be forgeries . . .

The effects of yesterday's raids have proved worse that had been expected. Everywhere buildings are lying in ruins. The Hospital of the Transfiguration was set on fire . . . Five doctors and several Red Cross nurses lost their lives. An emergency hospital is also in flames."

Polish journalist Stanislaw Balinski witnessed the bombing of Warsaw, Poland, in 1939.

Right: *Adolf Hitler (on right) receives bouquets from three boys in the newly merged Austria during a visit in 1940.*

the raw materials they needed as well as a market to sell their goods. In September 1931, the Japanese army invaded the part of China called Manchuria. Back in Japan, the army began to control the government.

Germany was strongly affected by the Depression as well. The economic situation helped a new political party, called the National Socialist German Workers' Party—or Nazis—rise to power. Adolf Hitler led the Nazis. The Nazi Party gained much power in the 1930s. In 1933, Hitler became the head of the German government and soon became dictator. He then began building up Germany's armed forces. Hitler believed that Germany needed more space and began taking over land around him. In 1938, he forced Austria to merge with Germany. In March 1939, he took Czechoslovakia. Then he turned his eyes to Poland.

WAR BEGINS

The war in Europe began on the morning of September 1, 1939, when German forces crossed the eastern border of Germany and attacked Poland. Many government leaders in Europe had predicted that the Germans planned to invade Poland at some point. In fact, after the Germans conquered Czechoslovakia, the British and French governments promised to come to Poland's aid if it were invaded. Hitler did not believe that they would keep their promise, so he went ahead with his plans. The attack on Poland introduced the world to a new type of warfare called "blitzkrieg" or "lightning war." German tanks and planes smashed Polish defenses, and the German army moved swiftly through Poland. German troops approached Warsaw, the Polish capital, within a week.

POLAND DEFENDED

The British and French governments kept their promise. They demanded that Germany withdraw from Poland. Hitler did not respond. On September 3, Britain and

Above: *Crowds wait outside Shanghai's City Hall in 1946 to welcome Chinese General Chiang Kai-Shek on his return for the first time since the Japanese occupation of 1937.*

TIME LINE 1935–1936

March 16, 1935
Military conscription introduced in Germany.

March 7, 1936
German troops march into the Rhineland.

October 1, 1936
General Francisco Franco becomes dictator of Spain.

October 25, 1936
Rome–Berlin "Axis" formed.

Above: *British prime minister Neville Chamberlain gives a radio announcement that Britain is at war with Germany.*

France declared war on Germany, but it was too late to save Poland. On September 17, the Soviet army marched across its western border and attacked Poland from the east. By September 20, all of Poland was either in German or Soviet hands. Hitler and Stalin, the leader of the Soviet Union, had made a secret deal not to attack each other and to divide Poland between them. Hitler never planned to keep his side of the pact.

THE START OF THE WAR IN ASIA

When the superior Japanese forces conquered Manchuria in 1931, the Chinese had to accept that Japan controlled part of their country. On July 7, 1937, Chinese and Japanese forces clashed near Beijing in what became known as the "Marco Polo Bridge Incident." China and Japan continued fighting until the end of WWII in 1945. The Japanese swiftly conquered much of northern China and the Japanese navy successfully blockaded the Chinese coastline. By 1938, southern China also fell into Japanese hands. The Japanese army halted in the mountains of central China. Although the Chinese fought a guerrilla campaign behind Japanese lines, a stalemate developed.

> "I was standing in the Wilhelmplatz about noon when the loudspeakers suddenly announced that England had declared itself at war with Germany. Some 250 people were standing in the sun. They listened attentively to the announcement. When it was finished there was not a murmur. They just stood as before. Stunned. The people cannot realize yet that Hitler has led them into a world war.
>
> "On the faces of the people . . . astonishment, depression. Until today, they have been going about their business pretty much as usual. There were food cards and soap cards, and you couldn't get gasoline, and at night it was difficult stumbling about in the dark. But the war in the west has seemed a bit far away to them."
>
> **CBS radio correspondent William Shirer's report from Berlin on September 3, 1939—the day France and Britain declared war on Germany.**

Above: Hitler explores conquered Paris, France. The iconic Eiffel Tower is in the background.

The war in Europe began in the east as Germany invaded Poland. The conflict then turned westward as German troops swept into other countries, including France, Norway, and Belgium. Britain stood alone fighting against Germany, withstanding huge bombing raids on its major cities. The United States was reluctant to become directly involved in another large-scale conflict. That sentiment changed on December 7, 1941. Japanese planes attacked the U.S. Naval base at Pearl Harbor, Oahu, in Hawaii. The war had moved out of Europe. It was now a global conflict.

"When all was clear and we were on the outskirts of Dunkirk, we stopped on a long raised road with the canal on either side and nice big trees sheltering us from the air. We got out and looked up—there were about seventy bombers knocking hell out of the docks or what was left of them. . . . the beaches . . . were black with troops waiting to go aboard, only there were no boats. They gave us a raid this afternoon and evening and the following day they gave us a raid that lasted from dawn till dusk, about seventeen hours. The fellows laid down on open beaches with the bombs falling alongside us, lucky it was sand, it killed the effect of the bombs."

British soldier Jack Toomey wrote this letter two weeks after his evacuation from Dunkirk, France.

GERMAN EXPANSION

After the Germans had successfully conquered Poland, Europe entered a period known as the "Phony War." Although Britain and France were officially at war with Germany, no battles occurred. Hitler had, however, ordered his generals to plan some attacks. The Phony War ended on April 9, 1940, when Germany invaded the Scandinavian countries of Denmark and Norway. Germany wanted to control the seaports and waters of the North Atlantic and wanted to establish air bases in Norway. Denmark surrendered almost immediately. British and French troops came to the aid of the Norwegians. While this action slowed the German advance, the result was never in doubt, and Norway fell. Britain and France expected Germany to attack France next by sending troops through neighboring Belgium. Instead, Germany launched its attack through the Ardennes Forest south of Luxembourg. Britain and France never expected combat troops

Above: Norway was a strategically important country for Germany to conquer.

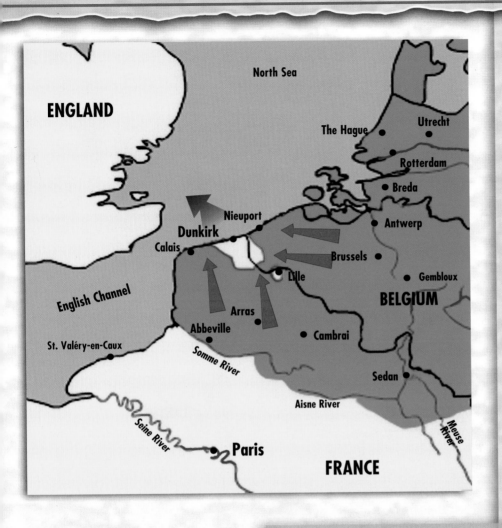

North Sea

ENGLAND

The Hague •   Utrecht •

Rotterdam •

• Breda

Nieuport

Dunkirk •   Antwerp •

Calais •

Brussels •   Gembloux •

• Lille

English Channel   **BELGIUM**

Arras •

Abbeville •

St. Valéry-en-Caux •   • Cambrai

Somme River

Sedan •

Aisne River

Seine River   **Meuse River**

Paris •

FRANCE

TIME LINE
1937–1939

May 28, 1937
Neville Chamberlain becomes prime minister of England.

July 7, 1937
Full-scale war erupts between China and Japan.

March 12, 1938
Germany invades Austria.

October 15, 1938
German troops occupy Sudetenland, Czechoslovakia.

March 15–16, 1939
German troops occupy the rest of Czechoslovakia.

March 28, 1939
Spanish Civil War ends.

Left: *British and French troops were evacuated from the northeastern port of Dunkirk, France. The blue arrow represents Allied forces and the red arrows Axis troops.*

and tanks to tromp through woodlands, and so they defended the Ardennes only lightly.

TOWARD DUNKIRK

The attack began on May 10, 1940. German tanks and soldiers smashed through the Ardennes, taking the French and British by surprise. On the same day, German airborne troops landed in the Netherlands and Belgium. The Dutch army surrendered on May 14, hours after a heavy bombing raid on the city of Rotterdam, the Netherlands. The German troops had advanced so

"First shock—the streets are utterly deserted, the shops closed, the shutters down tight over all the windows. It was the emptiness that got you. . . . Everyone lost his head. The government gave no lead. People were told to scoot, and at least three million of the five million in the city ran, ran without baggage, literally ran on their feet towards the south. . . . The inhabitants are bitter at their government. It even forgot to tell the people until too late that Paris would not be defended.

"Most of the German troops act like native tourists, and this proved a pleasant surprise to the Parisians. It seems funny, but every German soldier carries a camera. I saw them by the thousands today, photographing Notre Dame, the Arc de Triomphe, the Invalides."

American journalist William Shirer witnessed the fall of Paris, France, in June 1940.

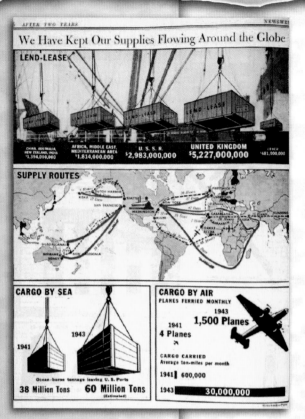

AFTER TWO YEARS

We Have Kept Our Supplies Flowing Around the Globe

LEND-LEASE

CHINA, AUSTRALIA, NEW ZEALAND, INDIA $1,394,000,000 — AFRICA, MIDDLE EAST, MEDITERRANEAN AREA $1,814,000,000 — U.S.S.R. $2,983,000,000 — UNITED KINGDOM $5,227,000,000 — OTHER $481,000,000

SUPPLY ROUTES

CARGO BY SEA
1941 — 38 Million Tons
1943 — 60 Million Tons (Estimated)
Ocean-borne tonnage leaving U.S. Ports

CARGO BY AIR
PLANES FERRIED MONTHLY
1943 1,500 Planes
1941 4 Planes
CARGO CARRIED
Average ton-miles per month
1941 600,000
1943 30,000,000

Above: *Poster promoting U.S. aid to the war effort, called "Lend-Lease."*

Above: *The British Spitfire (foreground) helped win the air battle against German planes such as the Messerschmitt Bf 109 (shown in the distance).*

quickly that by May 26, the British and French armies were surrounded at Dunkirk on the northeast coast of France. For the next two weeks, British and French troops were evacuated from the Dunkirk beaches and shipped to England. Belgium surrendered on May 28. The French army was ineffective against the German advance, and the Germans marched into Paris on June 14. On June 17, French leader Marshal Pétain offered to negotiate with the Germans. He signed the Franco-German Armistice on June 22. Germany was given complete control of northern France and the Atlantic coast. Pétain then set up a new French government in Vichy in southeast France. The Vichy government ruled that part of France until the Allies liberated the country in 1945.

BRITAIN ALONE

From June 1940 onward, Hitler controlled much of Europe. He had conquered Poland and successfully defeated Norway, Denmark, the Netherlands, Belgium, and France. Britain was the only country that still faced the might of Hitler's forces. The situation looked hopeless. When the British retreated from Dunkirk, they left behind nearly all their weapons and equipment. A few months earlier, Winston Churchill had replaced

"Tonight, I am appealing to the heart and to the mind of every man and every woman within our borders who loves liberty. I ask you to consider the needs of our nation and this hour, to put aside all personal differences until the victory is won. The light of democracy must be kept burning. To the perpetuation of this light, each of us must do his own share. The single effort of one individual may seem very small. But there are 130 million individuals over here. And there are many more millions in Britain and elsewhere bravely shielding the great flame of democracy from the blackout of barbarism. It is not enough for us merely to trim the wick, or polish the glass. The time has come when we must provide the fuel in ever-increasing amounts to keep that flame alight."

President Roosevelt addressing U.S. citizens about the Lend–Lease Act that he had just signed.

Neville Chamberlain as prime minister of Britain. Churchill was an inspirational war leader. His determination and rousing speeches made the British determined to fight on after so many defeats. Some people in the British government wanted to negotiate with Hitler, but Churchill believed that the British would never be defeated.

ATTACK FROM THE SKIES

With the fall of France, Hitler began making plans for the invasion of Britain. That meant crossing the English Channel, and this could not be done until the British Royal Air Force was destroyed. In August 1940, the Battle of Britain began with German air attacks on ports and airfields. The Royal Air Force (RAF) had an

"Paid visit to town and was on my way home by train when a flight of planes roared overhead. There came a series of explosions followed by a continuous rattle like pebbles falling on galvanised steel sheeting. The train pulled into a suburban station, the porters shouting 'Air Raid—Take Cover.' This was the real thing. Passengers poured calmly out of the subway. . . . Going out on to the platform, I joined a small group gazing into the sky. . . . The sky was blue and almost cloudless. There were puffs of bursting shells, the rattle of machine guns and the tiny shapes of our own interceptor planes darting into the swarm."

The diary entry of an unknown Londoner describes a fight during the Battle of Britain.

TIME LINE 1939

August 23, 1939
Nazi-Soviet nonaggression pact signed.

September 1, 1939
Germany invades Poland.

September 3, 1939
Britain and France declare war on Germany.

September 17, 1939
Soviet Union invades Poland in accordance with the Nazi-Soviet Pact.

September 27, 1939
Warsaw, Poland, falls to the Nazis.

Below : *During the bombing of Britain, children were evacuated from the cities to the relative safety of the countryside.*

Left: *In 1940, Winston Churchill became prime minister of Great Britain. His radio speeches strengthened the nation's determination to win the war against the Axis countries.*

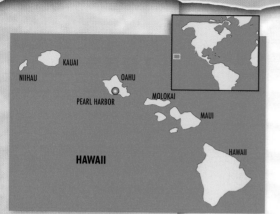

Above: *The U.S. base at Pearl Harbor, Oahu, is located in the Hawaiian Islands in the central Pacific Ocean. The islands became a U.S. territory in 1900. Hawaii became the fiftieth U.S. state in 1959.*

Below: *After the attack on Pearl Harbor, President Franklin D. Roosevelt led the United States into World War II.*

advantage over its German opponents. A new technology called "radar" gave the British advance notice of German air attacks. Britain could send its planes to meet the Nazis. By September 1940, Hitler realized that he could not defeat the British in the air. He postponed his invasion plans but ordered intense bombing raids on British towns and cities. These raids were called the blitz, short for blitzkrieg. The blitz began in London, England, on September 7, 1940. More than four hundred died. London was attacked many times until bombing ended in May 1941. Other British cities were also heavily bombed.

"Yesterday, December 7, 1941—a date which will live in infamy—the United States of America was suddenly and deliberately attacked by the naval and air forces of the Empire of Japan . . . Always will we remember the character of the onslaught against us . . . this form of treachery shall never endanger us again. I ask that the Congress declare that since the unprovoked and dastardly attack by Japan on Sunday, December 7, a state of war has existed between the United States and the Japanese Empire."

President Roosevelt addressed American citizens the day after the attack on Pearl Harbor.

TOWARD A WORLD WAR

Throughout the early years of what became World War II, the American government remained neutral. This policy was known as "isolationism." After World War I, many Americans did not want to involve the United States in fighting between other countries. Despite this, the United States helped the British in their resistance against Germany. Although the United States was officially a neutral country, there was a lot of public support for the British. In March 1941, the U.S. Congress passed the Lend-Lease Act. It allowed Britain to buy or rent weapons and other military equipment from the United States. Americans also worried about the expansion of Japanese influence. The United States government did not sell the Japanese steel, iron, or fuel for planes. Starting on July 25, 1941, the U.S. also prevented Japanese access to any money that they held abroad. The Japanese could not buy any metals or fuel. This policy brought the Japanese armed forces to a standstill.

Above: *The Blitz decimated parts of London, including this section of the East End.*

Above: *A monument to the USS* Oklahoma *on the grounds of the United States Capitol.*

HORROR IN HAWAII

In response to these strict sanctions, Japan began formulating a plan. It decided to attack the American Pacific Fleet at Pearl Harbor, Oahu, in Hawaii. Japan believed that, if it attempted to take over more of Asia, the U.S. would use those ships against them. Early on December 7, 1941, Japanese aircraft attacked the fleet at Pearl Harbor. The unexpected attack killed 2,403 Americans, including sixty-eight civilians. Many more were wounded. In less than two hours, the Japanese had either destroyed or damaged eight battleships, three cruisers, and three destroyers. The Japanese lost fewer than thirty aircraft, but the United States lost four hundred aircraft. On December 8, President Roosevelt spoke to the American people and declared war on Japan. Three days later, on December 11, 1941, Italy and Germany declared war on the United States. The war was now being fought around the world.

TIME LINE
1940

April 9, 1940
German army invades Denmark and Norway.

May 10, 1940
Germany army invades France, Belgium, Luxembourg, and the Netherlands; Winston Churchill becomes British prime minister.

May 15, 1940
Holland (the Netherlands) surrenders.

May 26, 1940
Troops rescued from Dunkirk.

June 14, 1940
Nazis take control of Paris.

June 22, 1940
France surrenders.

July 10, 1940
Battle of Britain begins.

September 7, 1940
German "blitz" on British cities begins.

Above: *The Japanese attack on Pearl Harbor lasted about one hour and fifteen minutes.*

"Men were screaming and trying to get aboard our ship and get out of the water. When I got to my gun, there were a few of the others there. We threw the gun cover over the side of the gun tube. And stood there cussing and crying at the Japs! You would be scared for a while and then you would get mad and cuss. After a while we finally got ammo up to our gun. But we had to put it into clips before it could be fired. I don't know how long a time this was. But the *Oklahoma* had rolled over on her side. And the harbor was pretty well afire by this time. The smoke and the fire was all around us. Then somebody yelled, 'Planes overhead!' We trained the gun around and started firing. One of the planes fell in front of Ford Island. I don't know who hit it, but it was one down."

Seaman Harlan Eisnaugle describes the Japanese attack on Pearl Harbor.

Right: *Soviet soldiers were used to fighting in icy conditions, a factor which initially helped them repel Hitler's army.*

W hen the Germans were confident that they had secured control of Western Europe, they turned their attention toward the richest prize of all: The Soviet Union. The German attack on the Soviet Union seemed unstoppable. It was finally halted at the gates of Moscow.

STALIN AND HITLER

Nazi Germany and the Soviet Union had signed a nonaggression pact in August 1939. Stalin believed that Hitler wanted to invade the Soviet Union. He thought that this pact would give him time to build up Soviet forces. Hitler signed the pact to ensure that he could invade Poland without interference from the Soviet Union. He never intended to stick to the agreement. He merely considered the pact a useful tool to keep the Soviet Union quiet while Germany dealt with Poland and conquered Western Europe. Once that happened, Hitler began planning his attack on the Soviet Union.

SPACE TO GROW

Hitler believed that the German people needed what was called *lebensraum* or "living space." He felt that the German empire needed to expand eastward into Poland and the Soviet Union. Hitler looked upon the people who lived in those territories as inferior to the Germans. The attack on the Soviet Union, known as "Operation Barbarossa," began on June 22, 1941. In the months prior to that date, Stalin refused to send his troops near the German border to avoid annoying Hitler. Now the Soviet army found itself unprepared for what became the largest attack in the history of World War II. More than three million German troops crossed the Soviet border on that day. They met little resistance.

VICTORY IN RUSSIA

The tactic of "blitzkrieg," which worked so well in Poland and Western Europe, was again used in this attack. The German army swept into the Soviet Union, covering vast distances in only a few weeks, and capturing more than one million Soviet troops. Hitler was determined to take the cities of Leningrad and Moscow before the end of 1941. He ordered his troops to push forward. By September, the German army was less than twenty miles from Moscow and just outside Leningrad when

Above: *Members of the Soviet army turned every building into a fortress as they fought to defeat the Germans at Stalingrad.*

they halted. The freezing winter had begun to set in, and the Germans were not ready for it. German troops besieged Leningrad for nine hundred days but did not succeed in taking it. Moscow, too, held out. The Soviet Union had begun the task of pushing back the German army.

JAPAN ADVANCES

The attack on Pearl Harbor on December 7, 1941, was only the start of a grand

Right: *German troops parade prisoners through the streets of Moscow.*

Japanese plan to dominate the Pacific and large areas of Asia. The Japanese attack was quick and relentless, but just like the Germans, the Japanese were eventually slowed

Above: *An anti-Soviet poster issued by the Nazi party.*

"After the news, I ran out to the street. Panic was spreading across the city. People hastily exchanged a few words, then rushed to the shops, buying anything they saw. They were running in the streets like mad. Many went to the savings bank to take out their deposits. This wave absorbed me, too. I also tried to receive cash from my savings bank. But I came too late. The bank was empty, payments had been stopped . . . Only in the evening everything became strangely quiet. It seemed that everybody had hidden somewhere, possessed by terror."

Elena Skriyabina writes in her diary about the way people in Leningrad reacted to the news of the German invasion.

TIME LINE
1941

March 11, 1941
Lend-Lease Act signed.

April 6, 1941
German Army invades Yugoslavia and Greece.

June 22, 1941
Hitler launches "Operation Barbarossa," the invasion of the Soviet Union.

June 28, 1941
Germans capture Minsk. Stalin later launches the "Scorched Earth" policy.

Above: *The British battleship* HMS Repulse *sank the German* Bismarck. *The* Repulse *was in turn sunk by Japanese airpower while trying to relieve Singapore on December 10, 1941.*

down and finally stopped. When the Japanese offensive began, both Britain and the United States controlled parts of Asia and the Pacific. They took action to protect their territories. Their actions proved too little, too late. Only weeks after Pearl Harbor, the Japanese took the Pacific islands of Guam and Wake from the United States. On Christmas Day 1941, British-held Hong Kong fell to Japan. In February 1942, a small Japanese army defeated a far larger British force in Singapore, in what was seen as one of the greatest failures in the history of the British army. In March, Japanese forces invaded Burma, and tens of thousands of refugees fled north to the border with India. Dutch-held Java surrendered under air and land attack, and one hundred thousand U.S., Dutch, British, and Australian troops were taken prisoner. The attack on the U.S.-held Philippines began on December 8, 1941, with bombing raids. Two weeks later, the land attack by Japan began. U.S. troops fought well, but surrendered on the Bataan peninsula on April 9, 1942. On May 6, 1942, U.S. and Filipino troops surrendered on Corregidor Island.

"The tank was hit and the plane caught fire so I jumped. I had to parachute from dangerously low down, but I survived. The parachute opened with a bang and I hurtled to sea. When I looked around, I saw three pillars of smoke far away. I later learned that our three aircraft carriers, *Akagi*, *Kaga*, and *Soryu*, had been destroyed. . . . I thought it was all over. We had no carriers to counterattack. There was nothing we could do."

Pilot Iyozo Fujita fought at both Pearl Harbor and the Battle of Midway. This extract was written after the Battle of Midway.

"The weird noise is the first thing that I remember about the jungle . . . . The birds sounded like dogs barking, . . . and the men were jittery initially when they first got there. They were shooting at everything that moved, but I finally convinced my squad that we didn't have much ammunition, that they couldn't waste any."

 U.S. soldier Kerry Lane recalls arriving on a Pacific island to fight the Japanese.

FIGHTING AT SEA

Japanese military leaders decided to conquer even more territories. They focused on Port Moresby in New Guinea. The first-ever "air-only" battle occurred on May 7 and 8, 1942, when Japanese and U.S. planes fought the Battle of the Coral Sea. U.S. and Japanese ships never saw each other; the entire battle took place in the sky above the Pacific Ocean. Japan did not capture Port Moresby. In the first week of June, a Japanese aircraft carrier fleet attacked Midway Island, about 994 miles (1,600 kilometers) northwest of Pearl Harbor. The Japanese believed that the American losses at Pearl Harbor meant that the U.S. had only a small fleet left to defend Midway Island. Meanwhile, the U.S. had broken Japanese codes and knew about the attack. On June 4, 1942, U.S. planes destroyed three Japanese aircraft carriers in five minutes and a fourth one later that day. The Japanese never recovered from this massive defeat.

WAR IN THE AIR

World War II was fought in a way that was completely different from any other conflict in history. For the first time, fighting in the air played a central part in the results of many battles. The battles of Britain, the

Above: *A Japanese reenactment of the British surrender at Singapore.*

Below: *Japanese troops celebrate victory in Hong Kong in 1941.*

TIME LINE 1941

September 8, 1941
Siege of Leningrad begins.

December 7, 1941
Japanese attack naval base at Pearl Harbor. United States and Britain declare war on Japan the next day.

December 11, 1941
Germany declares war on the United States.

"The Japanese army fed off the Philippines. They didn't bring any supplies; they ate up what we had grown for us to eat, so there was a lot of hunger and despair . . . . They were very cruel, even to passersby in the street. They would slap you down if you didn't greet them, if you didn't bow profusely enough, and there was a lot of hardship."

Carmen Guerra Nakpil remembers how the Japanese behaved once they conquered the Philippines.

Left: *A U.S. Marine pin.*

> "The hospitals were crammed. You could travel without a ticket on the train, bicycle on the pavements. There were no windows in the trains, no schools, no doctors, no telephone. One felt completely cut off from the world. There was no water, no light, no fire. Children collected wood from the ruins for cooking. Every family dug its own toilet in the garden."

Klaus Schmidt describes Darmstadt, Germany, after a British air raid in 1944.

Above: *Allied airplanes stage a wave of attacks over Berlin, Germany, during 1942.*

Right: *A U.S. bomber pilot prepares for the Battle of the Coral Sea in May 1942.*

Coral Sea, and Midway were all fought by aircraft. In the Pacific, aircraft not only fought each other, but also attacked ships. Both the U.S. and the British believed that heavy bombing of German and Japanese military and civilian targets would shorten the war. The United States produced huge numbers of aircraft for the war. Between 1940 and 1945, U.S. factories built more than three hundred thousand warplanes. Many were large bombers, such as the B-17 Flying Fortress and the B-29 Superfortress.

CITY ATTACK

The bombing of civilian targets was often called "carpet bombing." Although the Germans and Japanese also bombed towns and cities, Britain and the U.S. relied more on this tactic. In the last years of the war, the Allies bombed more than one hundred German cities, destroying nearly four million houses and killing almost one million civilians. Hamburg and Dresden, Germany, were almost completely destroyed. When U.S. bombers could finally reach the Japanese mainland, heavy bombing began. The Japanese suffered even more than the Germans because their houses were often wooden and built close together. Fires started by bombs spread quickly. On March 10, 1945, the U.S. staged an intense bombing raid on Japan. More than two hundred fifty thousand buildings

🎞 **FILM EXCERPT** 📖 **GOVERNMENT DOCUMENT** 🎙 **INTERVIEW/BOOK EXTRACT** 🎵 **SONG EXCERPT/POEM**

Above: *A reconstructed WWII airplane is currently on display in Sweden.*

Below: *German aircraft on the offensive over the Silvertown area of London's Dockland in the autumn of 1940.*

were destroyed and nearly one hundred thousand people died. Bombing raids also caused firestorms—rising columns of hot air and flames suck in cool air at ground level, which fans the flames, makes the fire burn hotter, and causes the air to rise even faster. It also creates winds so strong that the flames consume everything. Many people died in these firestorms throughout the war.

TIME LINE
1942-1943

April 9, 1942
Bataan Death March begins in the Philippines.

April 18, 1942
Colonel Doolittle's bombing raid on Tokyo launches from the USS *Hornet*.

May 30, 1942
Royal Air Force launches first one-thousand-bomber raid on Cologne, Germany.

January 10, 1943
Red Army begins siege of German-occupied Stalingrad.

February 2, 1943
German army at Stalingrad surrenders.

July 27–28, 1943
Allied bombing over Hamburg, Germany.

November 28, 1943
The "Big Three"—Roosevelt, Stalin, and Churchill—meet in Tehran, Iran, to plan the Normandy invasion.

"Suddenly there was a roar like an express train, a hurtling, a tearing, all-powerful overwhelming rush. Together we sprang to our feet. We got no further. The earth seemed to split into a thousand fragments . . . . Outside there was a stifling, forbidding atmosphere. I stumbled over two masses of debris, clattered over piles of glass. The moon shone wanly upon this uncanny nightmare. Women in the hall were dizzy. I rushed outside in the front. I saw at once all the windows of the flats had been blasted open or out."

Colin Perry describes an explosion that hit his parent's house during a German bombing raid over London, England, on October 18, 1940.

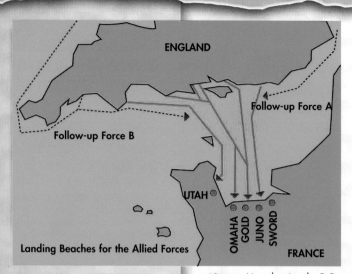

ENGLAND

Follow-up Force A

Follow-up Force B

UTAH

OMAHA
GOLD
JUNO
SWORD

FRANCE

Landing Beaches for the Allied Forces

Above: Map showing the D-Day invasion routes.

The end of World War II was several years coming. Allied troops slowly pushed back the German army from Eastern Europe, France, and Italy. The Allied D-Day landing was the largest military operation that ever occurred. In Asia and the Pacific, the Japanese fought to the death rather than suffer the dishonor of surrender. The United States finally used a devastating new bomb on two Japanese cities to bring World War II to an end.

BATTLE OF STALINGRAD

The German advance into the Soviet Union was halted outside Moscow. Neither the Soviet nor the German armies could defeat each other. In August 1942, Hitler ordered that Stalingrad be taken and diverted a huge army to attack the city. The Germans advanced into Stalingrad and were soon involved in fighting street by street. In November, Soviet forces encircled the city, trapping more than two hundred thousand German troops before attacking. Hitler ordered German troops never to surrender, but on February 1, 1943, the remnants of the German army caved in. The loss of Stalingrad signaled the beginning of the end for the Nazis.

D-DAY INVASION

By March 1943, the German army had been pushed out of North

> "We go to the centre of Stalingrad to bring some logs for the construction of the bunker. The impression from Stalingrad is terrible. A few stone buildings which had been there were razed to the ground during the air raid. Wooden buildings had been dismantled by the infantry to build bunkers, so that Stalingrad is completely in ruins. One can say that Stalingrad does not exist any more.
> It is 15 degrees below zero."

A diary entry from German soldier Heinz W. He was taken prisoner by the Soviet army.

Right: A soldier raises the Soviet flag over the Reichstag in Berlin, Germany, during the fall of the Third Reich in April 1945.

Africa, and in July, Allied forces invaded Italy. U.S. and British commanders knew they also had to liberate Western Europe. Allied forces planned an invasion on the Normandy Coast in northern France. On D-Day—June 6, 1944—Allied troops, headed by U.S. general Dwight D. Eisenhower, landed on the beaches of Normandy. It was the largest seaborne invasion in history and included an armada of about five thousand ships, such as steamers, merchant ships, warships, and landing craft. Paratroopers landed behind enemy lines shortly before the infantry hit the five landing beaches, code-named Utah, Omaha, Gold, Juno, and Sword. German resistance was strong, but by nightfall, the Allies held the Normandy Coast. Weeks of fierce fighting between the Allies and

Above: *Crowds flood the streets on VE Day, celebrating Germany's surrender in World War II.*

German troops followed. On August 25, U.S. and French Resistance forces liberated Paris. British and other Allied troops pushed northeast from Normandy into Belgium and the Netherlands. On December 16, 1944, a strong German force broke the U.S.-held front in the Belgian

TIME LINE
1944

January 6, 1944
Soviet Army advances into Poland.

January 27, 1944
Red Army breaks nine-hundred-day siege of Leningrad.

January 31, 1944
American forces invade the Pacific island of Kwajalein.

June 6, 1944
D-Day invasion in Normandy.

June 15, 1944
U.S. marines invade Saipan.

August 25, 1944
Paris liberated.

October 23–26, 1944
U.S. naval forces destroy remnants of Japanese navy in the Leyte Gulf, Philippines.

Left: *The Purple Heart is awarded to U.S. personnel wounded or killed during active duty.*

"'This is D-Day,' came the announcement over the British radio and quite rightly, 'This is the day.' The invasion has begun!

"Great commotion on the Secret Annexe! Would the long-awaited liberation that has been talked of so much, but which still seems too wonderful, too much like a fairy tale, ever come true? We don't know yet, but hope is revived within us, it gives us fresh courage, and makes us strong again. . . .

" The best part of the invasion is that I have the feeling that our friends are approaching. We have been oppressed by those terrible Germans for so long, they have had their knives at our throats, that the thought of friends and delivery fills us with confidence."

An extract from the diary of Anne Frank. Anne was a Jewish girl who hid from the Nazi occupiers with her family in Amsterdam, the Netherlands. Eventually captured by the Nazis, Anne, her sister, and her mother joined the six million other Jews of Europe who died at the hands of the Nazis.

Above: *A building in Stalingrad burns during the German onslaught in August 1942.*

> "Some Japs crawled up in early morning and charged our foxholes. They crawled to within ten feet of one fellow and started yelling, 'Hey, Corpsman.' All they wanted was for some fellow to show himself so the Jap could throw a hand grenade in his hole. The kid saw him and killed him. When they pull banzai charge, they gather together in a big group and start yelling. Then some of their officers start waving swords above their heads and shout, 'Banzai, banzai!' Of course our guns cut them down like flies, Milly, but it is scary listening to them scream like that."

Letter from U.S. soldier to his wife about the fighting on Iwo Jima.

Right: *In a desperate effort to reverse the course of the war, the Japanese revived the name "Kamikaze." Airborne suicide missions—flown by pilots with just enough fuel for a one-way trip— crashed into U.S. ships in hopes of causing extensive damage.*

Ardennes, causing a "bulge" in Allied lines. U.S. forces were surrounded at Bastogne. When asked to surrender, U.S. general Anthony McAuliffe replied "Nuts!" It became a rallying cry as American units raced to the area. Patton's Third Army broke through the German encirclement of Bastogne from the south on December 26, 1944. By January 16, 1945, German forces had been routed. In the first few months of 1945, U.S., British, and Soviet troops crossed into Germany in a race to reach Berlin first. Soviet troops prevailed. On April 16, 1945, the Soviet Union began its attack on Berlin. Eight days later, the city was encircled. On April 30, 1945, Hitler killed himself as Soviet shells exploded around him. A week later, Germany surrendered to the Allies. The war in Europe was over.

JAPAN ON THE DEFENSIVE

The war in the Pacific Theater raged on. After the Battle of Midway, Japan fought a defensive war. Although the U.S. lost as many ships and planes as Japan, it replaced them far faster. The Japanese found themselves defending a large amount of territory with fewer and fewer weapons. In the summer of 1942, Japan occupied the island of Guadalcanal as part of the assault on Port Moresby, New Guinea. The U.S. attacked Guadalcanal on August 7, 1942, but it was not until February 1943 that the Japanese were finally cleared out. Starting in May 1943, U.S. forces began "island-hopping"—

Above: *The Japanese officially surrendered on the USS* Missouri *on September 2, 1945.*

TIME LINE
1945

February 4–11, 1945
Roosevelt, Churchill, and Stalin meet at Yalta Conference.

April 12, 1945
President Roosevelt dies; Truman becomes president.

April 30, 1945
Adolf Hitler commits suicide.

May 8, 1945
Victory in Europe (VE) Day.

August 6 AND August 9
U.S. drops atomic bombs on Japanese cities of Hiroshima and Nagasaki, respectively.

August 14, 1945
Victory over Japan (VJ) Day.

attacking some of the Japanese-held Pacific islands while skipping others. The U.S. planned to capture an island with an airfield from which to bomb the Japanese mainland. Japan's loss of Saipan in late July 1944 allowed the U.S. to establish such a base.

END GAME

The first major battle of 1945 in the Pacific Theater began when U.S. forces landed on Luzon in the Philippines to take back Manila, the capital. Japan fought back fiercely. In February, U.S. Marines landed on the Japanese island of Iwo Jima, a strategic base from which to protect U.S. bombers flying over Japan. The battle for Iwo Jima lasted just less than one month and cost the lives of more than six thousand Marines and more than twenty thousand Japanese. In June, 1945, the U.S. lost twelve thousand Marines during the capture of the island of Okinawa, Japan. One hundred ten thousand Japanese died. The U.S. knew many thousands of people would die in an invasion of the Japanese mainland. This was one of the reasons that President Truman agreed to drop atomic bombs on Hiroshima and Nagasaki. These bombs instantly leveled those two cities and killed about one hundred twenty thousand people in total. Japan surrendered informally on August 14, 1945. The war in the Pacific—and World War II itself—was over.

Above: *An atomic bomb dropped on Hiroshima, Japan, on August 6, 1945, caused horrific damage.*

"I can never forget the sight of those people. They were burnt so badly that they didn't look human. Half of their ears were gone and their eyes were crushed. They didn't look like human beings. A person next to me said in a strained voice, 'Help me! Give me water!' The next moment he was dead. Many people lost their hair, bled from their gums, got a rash on their bodies."

Suzuko Numata recalls when the atomic bomb fell on Hiroshima, Japan.

You never know who's on the wires!

BE CAREFUL WHAT YOU SAY

Above: *A British propaganda poster reminds citizens to beware of possible German spies in their midst.*

"1) In all reports, Warsaw is not to be described as a town but as a fortress.

"2) Where possible, shoot film on a larger scale than previously of Jewish types of all kinds from Warsaw . . . not only whilst working but also character studies. This material should lead to a strengthening of anti-Semitic instruction in our domestic policies and in foreign affairs."

Propaganda Instructions of the Reich's Propaganda Ministry in 1939.

Right *Joseph Goebbels (far right) was responsible for Nazi propaganda.*

World War II affected people differently than any previous war. Newsreels (short movies) showed what was happening almost immediately (for that time period). Governments used propaganda, or biased publicity, to keep people on their side. Everyone—military and civilian, young and old, male or female—seemed involved in the war effort. In times of war, the arts, including music, painting, poetry, theater, and cinema often flourish as a means for people to "escape"—at least for a while. This was also true during WWII.

PROPAGANDA

During World War II, governments wanted their own citizens to support the war effort. Propaganda is a kind of advertising that encourages people to believe certain things. It works in many mediums, such as movies, printed materials, or live broadcasts. Governments also used propaganda to weaken the enemy. For instance, both the Germans and British dropped leaflets from planes on each other's cities in attempts to convince people that they were on the losing side. Posters—eye-catching, colorful, and quick and easy to produce—became one of the best-known forms of propaganda during WWII. Different countries used different messages on their posters. The Germans warned of the menace

of Soviet communism. The Soviet Union appealed to the patriotism of its many different peoples. The British used images of the countryside to show people what they were fighting for.

THE ROLE OF BROADCASTING

Very few people had television in World War II, but most people had a radio. This meant that each country could broadcast propaganda to the enemy as well as to its own people. Germany's most famous broadcaster was William Joyce, known as "Lord Haw-Haw." His broadcasts were meant to make the people of Britain less willing to fight. An American–born Japanese woman, "Tokyo Rose," broadcast radio messages designed to discourage U.S. troops in the Pacific. The British Broadcasting Corporation (BBC) broadcast throughout occupied Europe, encouraging people to write the letter V (for victory) in Morse code, or dot-dot-dot-dash. Chalked Morse code "V" symbols appeared everywhere as an act of defiance against the German conquerors.

THE WAR IN MOVIES

World War II movies became popular during and after the war. Some depicted actual battle scenes and included heavy fighting, while others dealt with the war's effects on peoples' everyday lives. For instance, *Casablanca*, starring Humphrey Bogart and Ingrid Bergman—and now considered a movie "classic"—told the story of two lovers who had to leave each other to fight the Germans. Musicals,

Above: *Nazi poster depicts a demonic U.S. soldier captured by a serene-looking Adolf Hitler.*

Below: *William Joyce, known as Lord Haw Haw, was Goebbels' anti-British mouthpiece. He was captured at the Danish border near Flensburg, and was later tried and executed.*

TIME LINE
1946–1949

March 5, 1946
Churchill gives Iron Curtain speech.

October 1, 1946
First Nazis convicted of war crimes at Nuremberg Trials.

March 12, 1947
Truman Doctrine announced.

June 5, 1947
Marshall Plan passed in U.S.

May 15, 1948
Israel created.

October 7, 1949
East Germany created.
USSR tests atomic bomb.

"The terrific casualties suffered by Allied forces in the first ten days of the invasion, which show that the British government has not the slightest regard for the life of its soldiers, have been compared . . . with the useless slaughter of British troops . . . in the last war. British troops have been forced into tank traps . . . in such numbers that literally mountains of dead bodies have to be climbed over by those following behind."

German propaganda broadcast to British troops in France soon after D-Day.

Above: *The Glenn Miller Orchestra helped make "Moonlight Serenade" and many other musical numbers popular.*

comedies, and detective stories unrelated to WWII were also very popular.

THE WAR IN MUSIC

Music helped many people forget their troubles during WWII. Berlin-born actress and singer Marlene Dietrich was popular with both German and British troops. Vera Lynn broadcast songs in Britain and sang for troops in Europe and Asia. Glenn Miller was one of the most popular American bandleaders of the era. His big band tunes, such as "Chattanooga Choo Choo," were played in dance halls throughout the United States and Britain. Miller's small plane disappeared over the English Channel in 1944.

BOOKS AND THE WAR

Reading, especially of detective novels, was another popular pastime during WWII. British novelist Dorothy L. Sayers' hero was the upper-class detective Lord Peter Whimsey. In the United States, Dashiell Hammet's Sam Spade novels gained popularity. After the war, many people wrote about their wartime experiences, including Nobel Prize winner, Elie Weisel, a concentration camp survivor. In 1947, *The Diary of*

"Oh! I have slipped the surly bonds of earth
And danced the skies on laughter-silvered wings;
Sunward I've climbed and joined the tumbling mirth
Of sun-split clouds—and done a hundred things
You have not dreamed of—wheeled and soared and swung
High in the sunlit silence. Hov'ring there,
I've chased the shouting wind along, and flung
My eager craft through footless halls of air.
Up, up the long, delirious, burning blue
I've topped the wind-swept heights with easy grace
Where never lark, nor even eagle flew—
And, while with silent lifting mind I've trod
The high, untrespassed sanctity of space,
Put out my hand and touched the face of God."

 The poem "High Flight" by John Gillespie Magee Jr.

Right: *Casablanca (1942) is set in occupied Africa during the early days of World War II.*

Anne Frank, the story of a young Jewish girl who wrote about her experiences while hiding from the Nazis, and who died in 1945 in the Belsen concentration camp, was published. It is still a widely read work from WWII. "High Flight," a poem by Royal Canadian Air Force pilot John Gillespie Magee Jr., describes how he felt as he flew his missions. Magee, who had one British and one American parent, died in a midair collision on December 11, 1941, at the age of nineteen.

Right: *War movies were popular long after 1945. The Guns of Navarone (1961) tells of a British team sent to destroy a gun emplacement in occupied Greek territory.*

Far right: *Vera Lynn was one of Britain's premier WWII entertainers. She helped lift the spirits of the public during those difficult years.*

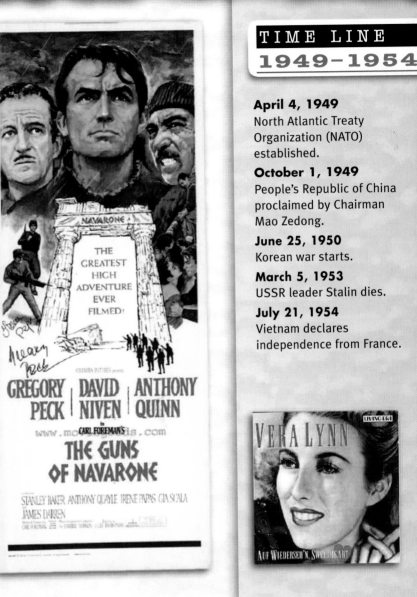

TIME LINE
1949–1954

April 4, 1949
North Atlantic Treaty Organization (NATO) established.

October 1, 1949
People's Republic of China proclaimed by Chairman Mao Zedong.

June 25, 1950
Korean war starts.

March 5, 1953
USSR leader Stalin dies.

July 21, 1954
Vietnam declares independence from France.

Rick: You have any idea what you'd have to look forward to if you stayed here? Nine chances out of ten, we'd both wind up in a concentration camp . . .

Ilsa: You're saying this only to make me go.

Rick: I'm saying it because it's true. Inside, we both know you belong with Victor . . . if that plane leaves the ground and you're not with him, you'll regret it . . .

Ilsa: But what about us?

Rick: We'll always have Paris. We didn't have, we, we lost it until you came to Casablanca. We got it back last night.

Ilsa: When I said I would never leave you.

Rick: And you never will. But I've got a job to do, too. What I've got to do, you can't be any part of, Ilsa . . .

Part of the script of *Casablanca*.

A s World War II drew to a close, the seeds of a new kind of conflict were sown. Those who had fought together separated into two different sides dominated by the United States and the Soviet Union. They did not fight each other directly, but this period was known as the "Cold War." In the twenty-first century, a new kind of conflict began with the September 11, 2001 attacks on the World Trade Center and the Pentagon.

Above: *Soviet premier Nikita Khrushchev (center) celebrates in Moscow's Red Square with cosmonauts Valentina Tereshkova and Valery Bykovsky on June 22, 1963. The two cosmonauts flew in separate spacecraft (Vostok 6 and Vostok 5, respectively) earlier that month. Their historic missions marked the first woman in space and the first time two manned spacecraft orbited Earth at the same time.*

Right: *After the Nazis were defeated, the Soviets took over much of Eastern Europe, including Czechoslovakia. This photograph is a reconstruction of the Russian entry into Prague, Czechoslovakia.*

A NEW KIND OF WAR

Since 1941, the United States, Britain, and the Soviet Union had fought together against common enemies. After the defeat of Germany and Japan in 1945, the Allies broke apart. The United States and the Soviet Union began regarding each other suspiciously. Stalin wanted to make sure Germany would never threaten him again. He made sure the countries bordering the Soviet Union had communist governments that he could control. The U.S. and the British wanted to stop the spread of communism and create democracies. Europe divided into a pro–American West and a pro-Soviet East. The mistrust between these two groups was called the Cold War.

"One of the primary objectives of the foreign policy of the United States is the creation of conditions in which we and other nations will be able to work out a way of life free from coercion. This was a fundamental issue in the war with Germany and Japan. Our victory was won over countries which sought to impose their will, and their way of life, upon other nations. I believe that it must be the policy of the United States to support free peoples who are resisting attempted subjugation by armed minorities or by outside pressures. I believe that we must assist free peoples to work out their own destinies in their own way."

In his March 12, 1947, address to Congress, President Truman stressed the duty of the United States to combat totalitarian regimes worldwide.

Above: *The Berlin Wall, erected in August 1961, became one of the most potent symbols of the Cold War.*

TIME LINE
1955–1975

MAY 14, 1955
Warsaw Pact created in response to NATO.

August 13, 1961
Work on Berlin Wall begins.

October 16–28, 1962
Cuban Missile Crisis.

March 8, 1965
First U.S. troops arrive in Vietnam.

June 5–10, 1967
Six-Day War in Middle East; ends with Israel gaining substantial territory.

January 27, 1973
Vietnam cease-fire agreement signed in Paris.

October 6, 1973
Yom Kippur War begins.

April 30, 1975
Vietnam War ends with unconditional surrender to the Vietcong.

TAKING SIDES

In Europe, the Cold War was most clearly seen in defeated Germany. It was divided between its occupying powers in 1945. Although Germany's capital, Berlin, sat in the middle of Soviet-occupied territory, it was also divided. In 1948, the Soviets blocked access to Berlin by road and rail in an attempt to drive out Britain, France, and the United States. They responded with massive airlifts that supplied their armed forces and fed the inhabitants of Berlin. The Berlin Airlift continued for fifteen months and focused worldwide attention on the situation.

In 1949, the United States, Canada, and Western European nations formed the North Atlantic Treaty Organization (NATO), a military alliance opposed to the Soviet Union—which responded with its own military alliance, the Warsaw Pact. The Soviet Union wanted East Germany, which it controlled, to be a separate country. Many people tried to escape to West Germany. In August 1961, the Soviets built the Berlin Wall to stop citizens from escaping. Troops from NATO and the Warsaw Pact faced each other across a divided Germany.

THE COLD WAR IN ASIA.

Between 1950 and 1953, communist North Korea and U.S.-backed South Korea fought in the Korean War. The Soviet Union and the United States

> "A lady saw my Berlin Airlift Veterans Association shirt. She stopped me and said, 'You are the first person I have ever met who participated in the Berlin Airlift and I would like to thank you for giving me life.' We had a little talk and she explained to me that she was a four-year-old when the blockade started. She got her first taste of chocolate from a candy bar dropped by the 'Candy Bomber.' We, the members of BAVA, firmly believe that the Berlin Airlift put the first big chink in the defeat of communism."
>
> **A former member of the Berlin Airlift Veterans Association.**

> "While the wall is the most obvious and vivid demonstration of the failures of the Communist system—for all the world to see—we take no satisfaction in it; for it is . . . an offense against humanity, separating families . . . and dividing a people who wish to be joined together. . . . Real, lasting peace in Europe can never be assured as long as one German out of four is denied the elementary right of free men, and that is to make a free choice. . . . this generation of Germans has earned the right to be free, including the right to unite their families and their nation in lasting peace."
>
> **President Kennedy speaking at the Berlin Wall on June 26, 1963.**

Above: *Jewish refugees arrive in Israel after its creation in 1948.*

also backed different sides in the Vietnam War, which lasted from 1965 to 1975 and ended in defeat for the United States. More than fifty-eight thousand Americans died in Vietnam.

BIRTH OF A STATE

After the end of World War II, many world governments supported the creation of the nation of Israel. The Nazis had killed at least six million Jews

Below: *A United States soldier tends to a wounded comrade during the Vietnam war.*

during the war, in what is known as the Holocaust. Land for a Jewish homeland was allocated from what was then Palestine, in the Middle East. Palestine had been controlled by the British since 1919, and many Jews already lived there. Israel was created officially in May 1948, but was immediately attacked by armies from Jordan, Egypt, Lebanon, Syria, and Iraq. The Israeli army fought off the attack, taking more territory in the process. Jordan and Egypt divided the rest of Palestine. In 1964, Arab governments set up the Palestine Liberation Organization (PLO) to coordinate efforts against Israel. In 1967, Israel fought the

Above On November 9, 1989, the German people destroyed the Berlin Wall.

February 17, 1979
China invades Vietnam.

December 24, 1979
Soviet invasion of
Afghanistan.

March 23, 1983
Reagan announces
"Star Wars" Initiative.

March 11, 1985
Mikhail Gorbachev
becomes president
of the Soviet Union.

December 8, 1987
U.S. and USSR sign
Intermediate-range Nuclear
Forces (INF) treaty banning
short- and medium-range
nuclear missiles in Europe.

**November–
December 1989**
Revolutions in
Czechoslovakia and
Romania oust communists.

Six-Day War against Arab nations, which nearly doubled the size of Israeli territory. Tensions in the Middle East heightened. In 1973, Egypt and Syria launched fresh attacks on Israel in the Yom Kippur War. Conflict in the Middle East continues to this day.

COLD WAR THAW

In 1985, the Soviet Union's new leader, Mikhail Gorbachev, wanted to make his country more open and democratic and end the Cold War. As part of this policy, some countries that had been controlled by the Soviet Union were allowed to be free again. In 1989, people throughout Eastern Europe took to the streets in a peaceful protest demanding freedom. There was little violence or conflict. Czechoslovakia's successful bid for freedom became known as the "Velvet Revolution." In Romania, there was savage

fighting, and its communist leader, Nicolae Ceausescu, was executed. One after another, Eastern European countries were freed from the domination of the Soviet Union. In November 1989, the Berlin Wall was opened. Thousands of East Germans streamed into West Berlin, and the East German government fell. By the end of the year, the two parts

Left: President Mikhail Gorbachev (1985–1991) wanted a more peaceful Soviet Union.

"The state of Israel will be open to the immigration of Jews from all countries of their dispersion; will promote the development of the country for the benefit of all its inhabitants; will be based on the precepts of liberty, justice, and peace taught by the Hebrew Prophets; will uphold the full social and political equality of all its citizens, without distinction of race, creed, or sex; will guarantee full freedom of conscience, worship, education, and culture; will safeguard the sanctity and inviolability of the shrines and Holy Places of all religions; and will dedicate itself to the principles of the Charter of the United Nations.

"In the midst of wanton aggression, we yet call upon the Arab inhabitants of the State of Israel to return to the ways of peace and play their part in the development of the State, with full and equal citizenship and due representation in its bodies and institutions—provisional or permanent.

"We offer peace and unity to all the neighboring states and their peoples, and invite them to cooperate with the independent Jewish nation for the common good of all."

Declaration of the Independence of the State of Israel, May 1948.

Above: *A Beijing citizen stands in front of tanks on the Avenue of Eternal Peace in Beijing on June 5, 1989, during the crushing of the Tiananmen Square uprising.*

Right: *After the terrorist attacks of September 11, 2001, U.S. planes, such as this one, attacked the Taliban government in Afghanistan. The Taliban supported perpetrators of the attack.*

REGIONS OF CONFLICT

In the Middle East, tension between Israel and its Arab neighbors continued. In 1987, the Palestinians launched an intifada, or massive uprising against the Israeli occupation. The intifada continued until 1993. Conflict also raged elsewhere in the region. In August 1990, Saddam Hussein, the leader of Iraq, invaded Kuwait. A coalition of armies led by the United States forced the Iraqis out of Kuwait in early 1991.

of Germany were reunited. Soon, the Soviet Union also broke apart. The Cold War had ended. The peaceful revolution was not universal, however, and communists still controlled China. Earlier in 1989, students began a protest in Beijing's Tiananmen Square, calling for more freedom. The government crushed the protest with troops and hundreds died between June third and fourth.

NEW ENEMIES

The worst terrorist attack in history occurred in the United States. On September 11, 2001, terrorists hijacked four aircraft and flew them toward different targets. One plane crashed in Pennsylvania before it reached its target. Another plane hit the side of the Pentagon in Washington, D. C. Two other planes targeted the twin towers of the World Trade Center, which

"Today I was feeling in the walking mood and decided to walk outside. I am located in World Financial Center 1. To get to me you need to be on the second floor of the twin towers to get on the internal bridge. But today I decided I would walk via the street.

"About two minutes after I got out to the street, I heard a loud explosion. I looked up and saw flames coming from the Twin Towers. I immediately thought it was a bomb. Debris was falling everywhere as if it were the ticker-tape parade for the Yankees. Suddenly I was hit in the head. I do not think it was a piece of the plane, I thought it might be office supplies because paper was floating down. But whatever hit me hurt me. I just turned around and ran across the street."

Richard Wajda worked at the World Trade Center on September 11, 2001.

FF

046

Above: Osama bin Laden, leader of al-Qaeda terrorists.

Above: The blazing south tower of the World Trade Center.

TIME LINE
1989–2005

June 3 and 4, 1989
China crushes Tiananmen Square revolt in Beijing.

November 9, 1989
Berlin Wall destroyed.

August 8, 1990
Iraq invades Kuwait.

October 3, 1990
Germany reunified.

October 15, 1990
Mikhail Gorbachev awarded Nobel Peace Prize.

December 26, 1991
Soviet Union dissolves.

September 11, 2001
Terrorist attacks on Pentagon and World Trade Center.

October 2001
U.S.-led coalition topples Taliban government in Afghanistan.

March 20, 2003
United States invades Iraq.

March 16, 2005
New parliament opens in Iraq.

collapsed. About three thousand people lost their lives. As a result, the United States and other countries began a war on terror. Osama bin Laden planned the September 11 attacks. He was hiding in Afghanistan. When the Afghan government, which was controlled by a group called the Taliban, refused to give him up, the United States bombed the country until the government fell—but bin Laden remains at large. The U.S. and its allies then began helping Afghanistan become more democratic. The United States attacked Iraq on March 20, 2003, under the belief that Saddam Hussein's government possessed weapons of mass destruction. Three weeks later, Saddam Hussein's government collapsed.

"Although Saddam has finally been captured . . . so far, interrogators are learning very little from him.

'What people have told me is that he, he's kind of out of it. Unreliable,' says Woodward. 'That he, at some moments, thinks he's still president. He's not in touch with reality, to the point where they can find what he says is reliable.'

" . . . while most doubt that Saddam still possessed any weapons of mass destruction, [President Bush] told Woodward he has no doubts at all about going to war."

Quotes from a *60 Minutes* interview of journalist Bob Woodward on April 18, 2004.

During WWII, millions of people throughout the world looked to their leaders as sources of inspiration and direction. Ultimately, however, the courage, sacrifices, and determination of everyday people thrown into extraordinary circumstances—whether or not they involved combat—shaped the outcome of the war. Some of the key players—Allied and Axis— who influenced events throughout WWII appear on these pages.

ADOLF HITLER (1889–1945)

Adolf Hitler headed the Nazi Party and was chancellor (leader) of Germany from 1933 to 1945. He became dictator of Germany, built up its military strength, and led the country into a war against Britain, France, the Soviet Union, and the United States. For a few years, his armies dominated much of Europe and North Africa. Eventually his actions resulted in defeat and ruin for Germany, the death of millions of people—including fourteen million prisoners—and the destruction and division of much of Europe. Hitler believed that Germans belonged to a superior "Aryan" race, and that this race should rule over "inferior" races, such as the Jews. He also believed that democracy threatened Germany's strength. He committed suicide just before WWII in Europe ended.

EMPEROR HIROHITO (1901–1989)

Hirohito was the emperor of Japan from 1926 until his death in 1989. He demanded that Japan surrender after the atomic bombs destroyed Hiroshima and Nagasaki. When the war ended, he helped the Allies turn Japan into a democratic nation. In 1946, Hirohito publicly denied his "divine" status. (Until then, Japan's emperors were considered deities.) In the 1970s, he toured the United States and Europe as a goodwill gesture. He died on January 7, 1989. His son, Akihito, became the new Emperor of Japan.

TOJO HIDEKI   (1884–1948)

Tojo served as prime minister of Japan from 1941 until 1944. In 1935, he commanded the Japanese army as it fought the Chinese in Manchuria. In 1938, he returned to Tokyo and became part of Japan's military government. He became minister of war in 1940. Two months before the attack on Pearl Harbor in 1941, he became prime minister of Japan. After the Allies occupied Japan, he was arrested as a war criminal. He was tried and executed on December 23, 1948.

JOSEPH STALIN (1879–1953)

Stalin's real name was Iosif Vissarionovich Dzhugashvili. He took the name Stalin, which means "Man of Steel," in 1910. After Lenin's death in 1924, Stalin headed the Soviet Union. He remained in power for twenty-four years. During that time, he ruled by terror. Millions died because of his actions. Stalin also took personal control of the Soviet armed forces during World War II, appealing to the Soviet citizens to fight against the Germans. As the war came to end, Stalin was determined that outside forces would never again threaten the USSR. He made sure that Soviet-friendly, communist-led governments were installed throughout Eastern Europe. His mistrust of Western Europe and the United States helped start the Cold War. Stalin died on March 5, 1953.

FIELD MARSHAL ERWIN ROMMEL (1891–1944)

Field Marshal Erwin Rommel was among the best-known German military commanders. Early in World War II, he commanded a tank division that pushed back British and French troops to the English Channel. Hitler promoted him to lieutenant general and gave him command of the Afrika Korps—the German soldiers based in North Africa. Rommel also inflicted a famous defeat over British forces at El Alamein in June 1942, a victory for which he earned the nickname the "Desert Fox" and a promotion to field marshal. Rommel commanded the German defenses in northern France and faced the Allied assault on D-Day. On July 20, 1944, Rommel played a minor role in a failed plot to assassinate Hitler. Rommel had the choice of standing trial or committing suicide. He killed himself on October 14, 1944.

GENERAL GEORGY ZHUKOV (1896–1974)

Georgy Zhukov became more and more powerful when he was put in charge of the defense of Moscow against the invading German army. When the threat to Moscow lifted, he began pushing back the Germans. Zhukov led the Soviet army to final victory over the Germans with the occupation of Berlin, Germany, in 1945, and then remained in Germany to lead the Soviet occupation of the eastern part of Germany. He returned in triumph to the Soviet Union in 1946. Stalin was jealous of Zhukov's popularity, demoted him, and sent him away from Moscow. After Stalin died in 1953, Zhukov returned to Moscow and became a leading member of the ruling Communist Party. He died in 1974.

WINSTON CHURCHILL (1874–1965)

Winston Churchill served as prime minister of Britain twice. In the late 1920s, he criticized the official policy of appeasement toward Hitler and fell out of favor with the Conservative Party. At the outbreak of war, however, he returned to government and soon became prime minister. During the rest of WWII, Churchill became known for his stirring speeches. In the summer of 1945, the Labour Party defeated the Conservative Party, and Churchill was no longer prime minister. In 1951, he was reelected and served as prime minister for four more years. He died ten years later, in January 24, 1965.

FRANKLIN ROOSEVELT (1882–1945)

Franklin Roosevelt was elected president of the United States in 1933, during the Great Depression. He offered U.S. citizens a "New Deal" to put people back to work. At the beginning of World War II, he kept the United States neutral. Roosevelt soon realized that Britain needed help fighting Nazi Germany. His Lend-Lease Act allowed the U.S. to supply the British with war matériel. Roosevelt brought the United States into WWII after the Japanese attack on Pearl Harbor. In January 1943, he agreed with Churchill that the only option for Germany and Japan was unconditional surrender. Roosevelt died on April 12 1945, roughly one month before the end of the war in Europe.

HARRY S TRUMAN (1884–1972)

Harry Truman became president of the United States in 1945 after Franklin Roosevelt's death. Truman led the U.S. to victory over Germany and the end of WWII in Europe. He decided to use the two atomic bombs on Japan to end the war in the Pacific later that year. He presided as the U.S. entered the Cold War with the Soviet Union. His suspicions led to the "Truman Doctrine," a policy designed to contain the expansion of Soviet power around the world. Truman did this mainly through the Marshall Plan and the creation of NATO in 1949. He also sent troops to fight communists in Korea and provided help in the fight against Vietnamese communists. Truman retired in 1952 and died

ADMIRAL CHESTER WILLIAM NIMITZ (1885–1966)

Admiral Nimitz helped lead the Allied forces against Japan in the Pacific Theater of War. He served in World War I as a submarine commander in the Atlantic. During the 1930s, Nimitz rose through the ranks of the U.S. Navy. In December 1941, after the Japanese attack on Pearl Harbor, he became commander in chief of the U.S. Pacific Fleet. Nimitz was known as a great military thinker who was willing to take risks. He commanded U.S. forces during the Battle of Midway, the Coral Sea, the Solomon Islands, and others. The great success of the U.S. Navy in the Pacific Theater was due largely to his leadership. He died on February 20, 1966.

DWIGHT EISENHOWER (1890–1969)

In 1942, General Eisenhower became head of U.S. forces in Europe. He was Supreme Allied Commander of the Allied Expeditionary Force and led the D-Day invasion. As the Cold War with the Soviet Union began, he became Supreme Allied Commander of the North Atlantic Treaty Organization (NATO) troops. In 1952, he was elected president of the United States. He remained president until 1961. Under his presidency, the Korean War came to an end. Although a known opponent of the Soviet Union, Eisenhower hoped to establish a working relationship with the Soviet leadership. He died on March 28, 1969.

GENERAL DOUGLAS MACARTHUR (1880–1964)

General Douglas MacArthur commanded Allied troops in the Pacific and Asia. The Japanese invaded and conquered the Philippines while MacArthur was in command, and he retreated to Australia. With Admiral Nimitz, MacArthur led a combined U.S. and Australian force that gradually retook islands in the Pacific that were conquered and held by Japanese. With the surrender of Japan in September 1945, MacArthur was put in charge of the reconstruction of Japan. He helped create a democratic government and made sure that Japan would never again be a military power. In June 1950, he headed the United Nations Army in South Korea. He died on April 14, 1964.

alliance a cooperation of groups united for a common cause.

appeasement submissive behavior in the hope of resolving a conflict.

atomic relating to atoms.

Allies the United States, Britain, France, and other countries allied against Germany, Italy, and Japan.

Axis Germany, Italy, Japan, and other countries allied against the United States, Britain, and France.

Battle of the Bulge a fierce German offensive battle fought in the Ardennes Forest in late 1944–early 1945.

Battle of Britain the struggle for air supremacy over southern England in 1940–1941 between the British and German air forces.

Berlin Wall a barrier erected across the center of Berlin to prevent people in Soviet-held East Germany from escaping to West Germany.

blitz (short for blitzkrieg) an intense bombing attack by the Germans over Allied territories.

blitzkrieg German for "lightning war," an intense burst of bombing over a target.

broadcast a radio or TV program; to transmit information via airwaves.

carpet bombing dropping enough bombs in an area to cause uniform destruction.

civil war war between citizens of the same country.

civilian a person who is not a member of the armed forces.

coalition a temporary alliance formed for action against a specific problem.

Cold War name given to hostile relations between the United States and the Soviet Union and their respective allies; did not involve actual combat.

communism a social theory that advocates a classless society, the abolishment of private property, and collectively owned industries and land.

concentration camp a prison camp for people whom the authorities wish to remove or segregate from society.

conscription involuntary enlistment.

D–Day June 6, 1944; the first day of the Allied invasion of Europe in World War II.

democracy a form of government in which power is vested in the people and is administered by them or by their elected representatives.

Depression a period of massive worldwide economic turndown, especially during the 1930s; also known as the Great Depression.

front a battle line.

guerrilla a member of a force, usually operating in small groups, that engages in warfare with or harassment of an army.

hijack to steal something while it is in transit.

Holocaust the extermination of six million Jews (specifically) by the Nazis during WWII; the term *holocaust* has also been used in reference to the killing of as many as fourteen million people—including the Jews—deemed "undesirable" by the Nazis during WWII.

iconic relating to a symbol.

independent not relying on or being dependent upon others.

intifada the uprising in 1987 and continued Palestinian resistance to Israeli occupation of the Gaza Strip and the West Bank of the Jordan River.

Iwo Jima a hotly contested island in the Pacific.

kamikaze a Japanese suicide pilot; also, an attack by such a pilot.

lebensraum German for "living space," a Nazi policy that advocated taking over land in other European countries to increase German territory.

Lend—Lease Act a U.S. program that supplied weapons to countries fighting the Axis powers.

Nazi a member of an extreme political party, the National Socialist German Workers' Party.

negotiate discuss with the aim of reaching a mutual agreement.

Netherlands a kingdom in western Europe, divided into provinces, one of which is Holland.

Pacific Theater of War the WWII battle areas in and around the Pacific Ocean.

Pearl Harbor a naval base on the island of Oahu, Hawaii, that the Japanese attacked without warning on December 7, 1941. The attack destroyed much of the U.S. Pacific Fleet. The incident caused the U.S. to enter World War II.

PLO Palestine Liberation Organization, a group set up to fight Israel's occupation of Palestine. Originally a terrorist group, it renounced terrorism in 1988.

propaganda biased (one-sided) information aimed at influencing people's opinion.

Rhineland Germany west of the Rhine River.

Soviet Union, the Union of Soviet Socialist Republics (USSR) states making up one nation, of which Russia was the chief component. These republics, now independent nations, include Armenia, Azerbaijan, Belarus, Estonia, Georgia, Kazakhstan, Kyrgystan, Latvia, Lithuania, Moldova, Russia, Tajikistan, Turkmenistan, Ukraine, and Uzbekistan.

surrender to give up, especially when forced.

Taliban a religious group that ruled Afghanistan until the United States removed it from power after the terrorist attacks of September 11, 2001.

VE Day victory day in Europe, the official end of World War II in Europe: May 8, 1945.

Velvet Revolution a term applied to a revolution achieved without bloodshed—especially the revolution in Czechoslovakia.

VJ Day victory over Japan day, the official end of fighting in the Pacific Theater: August 15, 1945.

Please visit our web site at: www.garethstevens.com
For a free color catalog describing Gareth Stevens Publishing's
list of high-quality books and multimedia programs,
call 1-800-542-2595 or 1-800-387-3178 (Canada).
Gareth Stevens Publishing's fax: (877) 542-2596.

Library of Congress Cataloging-in-Publication Data

Hynson, Colin.
 World War II: a primary source history / Colin Hynson.
  p. cm. — (In their own words)
 Includes bibliographical references and index.
 ISBN-10: 0-8368-5983-9 ISBN-13: 978-0-8368-5983-6 (lib. bdg.)
 1. World War, 1939-1945—Juvenile literature. I. Title: World War 2.
II. Title: World War Two. III. Title. IV. In their own words (Milwaukee,
Wis.)
 D743.7.H97 2005
 940.53—dc22   2005046495

This North American edition first published in 2006 by
Gareth Stevens Publishing
A Weekly Reader Company
1 Reader's Digest Rd.
Pleasantville, NY 10570-7000 USA

This U.S. edition copyright © 2006 by Gareth Stevens, Inc.
Original edition copyright © 2005 ticktock Entertainment Ltd.
First published in Great Britain in 2005 by ticktock Media Ltd.,
Unit 2, Orchard Business Centre, North Farm Road, Tunbridge Wells,
Kent, TN2 3XF, U.K.

Gareth Stevens editor: Carol Ryback
Gareth Stevens art direction: Tammy West

Photo credits: (b) bottom; (c) center; (l) left; (r) right; (t) top
Aviation Photographs: 4–5(c), 24(t), 25(c), 28(b). CORBIS: 5(b), 7(b),
9(cr), 11(t), 12–13 (all), 18(b), 23(cr), 28(t), 29(cr), 34(b), 36 (all), 38(t),
39 (all). Everett Collection: 6–7(c), 32(c). Library of Congress: 8(b),
16(t), 18(b), 19(b), 24(b).

Printed in the United States of America

2 3 4 5 6 7 8 9 10 09 08 07

FOLGER McKINSEY ELEMENTARY SCHOOL